Eclectic Cowboy and Other Poems
___

Eclectic Cowboy and Other Poems

Sherry Bevins Darrell

Jennings Street Press
2019

Copyright © 2019 by Sherry Bevins Darrell

All rights reserved. This book or any portion thereof may not be reproduced or used in any manner whatsoever without the express written permission of the publisher except for the use of brief quotations in a book review or scholarly journal.

Cover art by Xinran Hu based on a photograph by George Payne.

First Printing: 2019

ISBN 978-0-9906516-3-5

Jennings Street Press
100 E. Jennings Street
Newburgh, IN 47630

To the eclectic cowboy himself, best muse of all,

George Payne.

Contents

Acknowledgements...1
Eclectic Cowboy..3
Back in Black Suit...7
On the Prairie...9
Full Moon Art, Full Moon Heart..................................13
Homeward..17
My Love Goes to Texas...19
Prayer for Her Son..21
Stoic Stories...23
On His Knees..27
Four Musings..29
No Dancing with Trees...31
Beyond the Glass..33
Night Terrors...35
Cockroach Hopes...37
Diagnosis: Hole in Heart..39
Saint George and Three Dragons..................................41
Two Out of Three..43
Plundering Huns...45
Noble...47
Orogenies...49
Longing for Egypt...53
To Know...59

Wrestling with the Angels	63
In the Suburbs	65
Table Service	67
Arrivals	69
In the Dark	71
What Milton Knew	73
About the Author	76

Acknowledgements

My thanks for poem ideas resulting from two sermons at Trinity United Methodist Church: "To Know" from Todd Gile's sermon about how we do and do not know truth; and "Longing for Egypt" from Kaitlin Moore Morley's sermon on grumbling Israelites following Moses out of Egypt. Thanks, too, to Danny Trusty for insisting I write about plundering Huns.

My friend and colleague Xinran Hu, an award-winning book designer, kindly created the cover. Attorney, literary agent, and energetic, devoted friend Joshua Claybourn performed miracles, speedy miracles to ensure this wee book reached publication in a beautiful form. I owe Josh thousands of lunches.

Over the past few years, I have relied on wonderful friends to read and respond to various poems. For their patience and discernment in helping me think through poetic problems, solve most of them, edit lines, and eliminate whole sections, I owe great debts (perhaps payable in chocolate) to Charlotte Knapp, Becky Browning, Kathy Bartelt, Judy Buckman, Sharon Deaton Darrell, and especially Charmaine McDowell.

Finally, thank you to George for photographs and much, much more.

Eclectic Cowboy

I

Through the stock pen strides a quiet cowboy, dressed
according to custom: brimmed hat; long-sleeved,
wrinkle-free shirt; woolen vest
brown or charcoal best;
Wranglers or Levis pressed;
handmade leather chaps; leather gloves;
leather boots, today's brown with plain upper
and modest
tooling on the shafts.
First blanket, then saddle he lifts onto the Paint;
today they cut calves, a semiannual test
for this cowboy whose lifework (engineering oil and gas)
he leaves for this vacation—Texas rest,
for him the best
place for a guest
to indulge what he's obsessed
with: horses, horsemanship, horse lore.
This morning, his heart rides high as wind,
warm as October sun on canyon walls.
Here he'll work a week till mind, body, soul
feel refreshed.

II

Down the hall lopes a grinning cowboy, dressed
according to custom: button-down, long-sleeved
wrinkle-free, Brooks Brothers shirt; vest

buttoned snug, of brown or charcoal wool; his best
Wranglers or Levis pressed
to a sharp crease to match the toe
of leather boots, tonight's black with plain upper
and modest
tooling on the shafts.
His briefcase he sets square on the floor.
With easy grace, this cowboy shifts
among the Wallaces: Stegner, Stevens, Pratt.
Inside his saddlebag-substitute rest
the essentials: laptop and iPad;
reports on reservoirs, porosities,
production plans; the latest views expressed
on Jefferson and Lee.
And tonight the cowboy's brought
a paperback of poems wrought
about the owls' companion; AAPG's
Explorer—and always master horseman Xenophon.

III

In the kitchen this cowboy is pressed
to speak and read. At the cook's behest
he recounts some heroic rancher's geste,
some other cowboy's quest
for honor, justice, right.
Or perhaps he reads with high zest
a poem from Daniel Boone, addressed
to Brother Squire, about those owls who nest
high along the trace
and hoot him prayers each night,
owl-guardian-angels who sing his praise.

In the kitchen the cowboy's words and silence,
his rhythms and music express,
unknown to him, his own grace:
he carries the heart
of the world in his art.
But the cowboy just looks down,
engaged with text,
never guessing
that those waiting for each word
know he is both blessed
and blessing.

Bevinses' branding at Pitts Ranch, Borger, Texas, June 2017.
Photo by author.

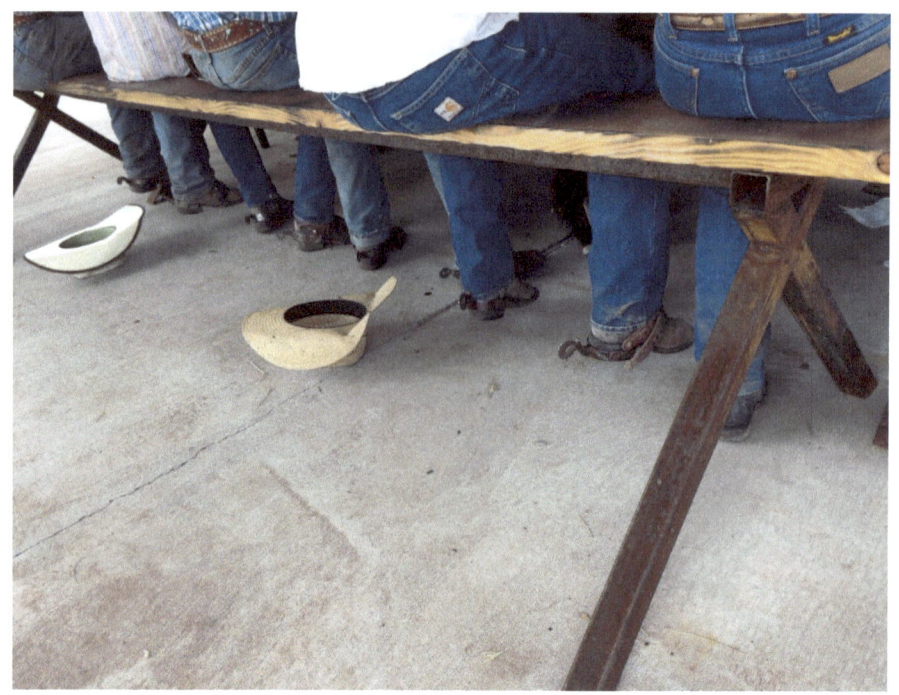
Tim Cooper's lunch after branding, Borger, Texas, June 2017.
Photo by George Payne.

Back in Black Suit

I saw him from the back
With a hint of profile,
Right ear turned toward the yack
Of those I, too, love.

Near the back, I just sat
And pondered this man: his back
Revealed taut muscles, but lack,
Oh, a great lack of kisses.

In minutes, he left the pack
And turned; I sat back
Alone, heart rising. What tack
To choose? Embrace? Dismiss?

O beautiful man in black
Who turns his fierce, kind back
On others, steps back
Where I wait. Embrace.

On the Prairie

"Labor omnia vincit . . . " Vergil, *Georgics*

I

Arriving over centuries, perhaps
across an ancient land bridge, perhaps harried
by cavalry or high on promises,
the brave came here, some on foot, some on horse,
and some in wagons:
Creek, Cherokee, Choctaw, Pawnee, others.
They dreamed of eagles and wolves
and slept under stars whose lives they knew.
Amidst black grama and tufted foxtail,
they read the rabbit's step and the shrew's squeal;
pinyon pines sang them to sleep.
The brave whetted spearheads, arrowheads, knives
of flint, obsidian--sharp, sharp, deadly.
Nomadic hunters, they cherished the plains
where roamed woolly bison who nourished them
till slain in millions, where grew prairie grass
high enough to hide a massacre,
where ended trails of weeping ones.

II

At seventeen, the brave came west alone,
strong, somber, set to discover what lay
beneath the plains. Across the Mississippi

he came to learn about Mississippian
and all other crucial strata.
Beneath Bizzell's high beams and pointed arches,
he labored, quiet, far from his tribe:
home, parents waited, brother watched to see
if this brave one survived, mastered the plains.
Already he had an ear for Dylan
and the Byrds and a heart for cowboys,
lonesome fellows prairie-bound, men who lived
under sun and stars, trust reserved for horses.
Already learned in the language of toil,
he spoke mathematics, formulae here
and, armed against ignorance, carried books,
pencils, slide rule to and fro, commuting
on foot six miles a day to class, library,
dorm, class, library, dorm—even Sundays
crossing up and down, back and forth
for prayer, hymn, psalm, body and blood, before
dorm, library, dorm. Amongst lecture halls
and book stacks, he explored old, old earth,
her aeons and ages lying hidden,
under the surface, where ever busy
she produced gas and oil Tau Beta Pis
and Sigma Taus would free her of.   Surrounding
the brave one, urging him to cherish
the west, her prairies and wide, flat plains,
old Cherokee dreams whispered from the heights.

III

And now, fifty years on, he walks there again,
surprised by pride rising in his heart: brave

he came at seventeen, matured beneath
prairie skies, ably carried away with him
earth's ancient and modern lore. Today man
and master, he returns, again quiet,
one whose wisdom others seek: a chief.

Rosenberger Lease, Kiowa County, Kansas, March 2016.
Photo by George Payne.

Full Moon Art, Full Moon Heart

> *Full Moon Lodge* describes "the relationship between mankind, Mother Nature, and the creator of the universe whose medicine is love. It acknowledges our place between the sun and the full moon."
> ~ Starr Hardridge

In myth the creator hangs sun and moon
like sparkly Christmas ornaments against
a dark-blue sky, orbs to set the tune
for music of the spheres.
In science our fat, hot sun swims
through her spiral galaxy, holds us tight.
Never her gravity wanes, nor her light dims.
In her possessive clutch our speedy flight
amazes us still, even in this season
of distance, when we lean away from her
into cold and dark; our reason
insists that if she looks pale and wan
through clouds, if she appears aloof,
unbothered by our distance from her
just now, that's merely proof
she can, like best parents, best lovers, let
us stray and keep us close yet.

In this same cool season, three super moons
hold us in awe, their lights gold, red, blue
(like Starr's paint), boons
predicted yet unexpected. All three rare,
warm friends, close and podge,
comfort and delight us while we dare
to glance from sheltering lodge
up at our cold, white sun.

Of course, Starr knows it's warmth we want--
O, let us dream beneath heavy blankets.
Thus, out there on Oklahoma prairie,
Muscogee Creek Starr sets a wide tepee
twixt sun and full moon, depicts
a universe in blue, gold, hot orange.
Beyond heavenly ornaments,
beyond heart's yearnings,
beyond mind's imaginings,
beyond brain's learnings,
Starr's creator, who set ardent sun
and amiable moon above
to illumine Nature and ourselves,
eternally breathes medicines of love
on all dwelling in this place.

Meanwhile, another prairie
son prizing soogans that stave off wind
and freeze, fear and lonesome carries
this heavy woolen beauty to warm
our lodge. May the creator gaze
on him, see how he, too, heals,
and wrap him all his days
in the sun's embrace.

Supermoon, north of Greensburg, Kansas, July 2014.
Photo by George Payne.

Homeward

Six hours northwest of Dallas,
We rise onto the caprock,
No more farms green with soybeans, cotton, maize
Sprouting from black furrows; no more pivots
Sprinkling fossil water over fields.

Up here, the land changes
To flat and brown and treeless.
A mile away, you can spot a clump
Of mesquite scrub or yucca. The sky is big, blue,
Brilliant--no trees or hills or clouds block the view.
On wired-in lands that pass for pastures,
Cattle graze, Herefords, their burnt-sienna hides
The same hue as earth. For rest and shade,
They congregate around wells pumping, pumping—
Incessant wheeze up and down for oil.

Eight hours. Barely past Amarillo.
From the west blow in black thunderheads—
To threaten, not to rain
On this parched earth. Instead, at fifty per,
Storm winds thrust dirt and tumbleweed
Across the road.

The last half hour homeward.
The scent of sour gas hails us; cattle and wells—
Dozens, hundreds in twenty miles—herald us on.
Baptized in that blue sky, this homely land
Is the closest place on earth to heaven.

Terry Bevins and Mac at sunrise on the Harvey Ranch, Hutchinson County, Texas, June 2017. Photo by George Payne.

My Love Goes to Texas

This week my love goes to Texas.
He drives west in a big, black truck,
festooned with toolbox on the back,
and taps his boots to NPR.

This week my love drives to Texas
where he hears Irish Celts sing and play
their dobros, banjos, mandolins,
American music acoustic.

This Alamo week, my love hears
in Texas Travis's epistle
read and re-read, and historians
examine Crockett and Bowie.

Somewhere in Texas, my love reads
and mulls Tillich, Borg, Josephus;
recalls the gestes of Charles Goodnight
and other heroic horsemen.

This week my love drives through Texas
counting the oil wells ducking down
and up and those others still and dry.
Across faint slopes, wind farms draw his eye.

In Texas this week my love loves
the canyons filled with pinks, reds, blues
and thunderheads black and booming
from an eternal, topless sky.

Home. Texas. Take my heart, my love,
with you. Let us hear the music;
let's stay and waltz and watch the light,
my love, when you go, this week, to Texas.

Celebrating Texas Independence, Acton, Texas, March 2017.
Photo by author.

Prayer for Her Son

(in memory of Ruth)

In hot late August, after one o'clock
she stands in dark, too pregnant to sleep,
first child restless in her belly,
hair damp and skin clammy.
When will my son come?

Over his crib she has pulled taut white sheets
and a light, square quilt, hand-sewn
in her mother's tiny, precise stitches.
Above hang red, blue, and yellow ABCs:
may my son read early and late and long.

Each morning she reviews his layette
sewn, knitted, crocheted, embroidered
by kinswomen and friends. She pats
undershirts and sleepers and socks.
She plumps the stack of soft white diapers
neatly folded beside three pairs of matching
diaper pins. She runs her fingers down
six shiny glass bottles sterilized
precisely as her mother taught.
May he always be warm, healthy, and safe.

These late days she rocks, imagining his weight
against her shoulder, her hand rising to pat his back,
smooth his downy hair. Through the window now
comes moonlight, reminding her to add a lamp,

some night light. *May he never fear the dark;*
may he never feel alone, afraid.

When she sits, she folds hands over her belly,
over her son, almost cradling him on her lap.
Her aunt insists he is a boy because
she carries high; the same aunt has stitched
his little shirts and shorts and overalls.
The drawers where they lie folded hold, too,
a pink dotted-Swiss dress with ruffles
and satin ribbon for a sash--that dress
came from a friend with less faith in lore.
The blue ball on the chest: she prays, *Someday*
let me watch this boy tossing his ball.
Let me kiss his wounds, swathe knees and elbows
in iodine and gauze. Let me hear him slam
the screen door as he rushes in with news
from school and Scouts. And when he sits, head bowed
over arithmetic, let me again
caress his neck, his soft hair. May I live
to witness his setting forth,
all the warmth of his breaths still on my cheek,
all the weight of his bones light in my arms.

Stoic Stories

I

Sobs seize the throat. The tight-jawed stoic
removes his spectacles and wipes his eyes.
He chokes and coughs, then wrestles loose the knot,
that huge bull standing on his tongue, stretching
down his throat. Long pause till an almost-word
escapes, an almost-name from Greek: *manly,
masculine*; disciple, saint, cross, son. Son.

II

At a funeral, some not-young woman,
clutching a newspaper clipping, thanks him.
For years she meant to thank those two men.
Four decades ago, enraged and broken,
out on the rig, a man knifed her father
in the back, near his heart. The brothers saved
him, gave her father back to her. Again
the stoic pauses, wrestles that familiar,
ferocious bull loose again. Finally,
two names erupt, father and uncle, who saved
a man—for a little girl, a daughter.

III

Two scenes revealed, but many to suppress
while eagles devour his liver and bulls
stifle his breath. He's right: he has watched

too many Westerns, admired too many strong,
lonesome men who chose frontiers other souls
dare not trespass. Riding the prairie alone,
he has become laconic, a man
of private, quiet grief such that his past
persists mostly in rumors and whispers.
He has wrestled countless bulls, pushed them down
his throat, swallowed, gulped, kept them deep within.

He has gritted and ground his teeth to live
as taciturn and fiercely proud as Call
and Goodnight. Thus he maintains the balance:
no hope and no despair, taking the world
as it comes—a stoic—while the eagles'
sharp beaks rend his liver; his flesh rips, bleeds.
No flinching. He gulps the bull back down.

Kiowa County, Kansas, August 2016. Photo by George Payne.

On His Knees

Mid-morning, a man drops to his knees
before an altar rail. Lean shoulders hold
burdens gladly borne for those he loves,
making their worlds better, his bearable.
Back straight, elbows bent, palms open
to accept bread and wine, he waits, communes,
then folds his hands, slender fingers lacing,
his head now slightly bowed and eyes pressed shut
in prayer.

What forgiveness can he possibly need,
this saint clad in brown practically a match
for capuchin's cassock? And what god does
he postulate and implore? From what god—
remote in unimaginable heaven
far above, beyond all stars, past billions
of galaxies stretching millions of light years
into present, past, future—does he seek
the grace his soul craves? What pardon can he need?
From what god—tender, infinitely close,
a whisper in the brain—does he beg help
for those omissions oppressing his mind?
What good can he have overlooked in that
diurnal endeavor to do all the good
he can?

He prays and waits, an expert at waiting.
How little he requires, of anyone,
of even god.

Four Musings

Checkers

Geez, I am too old for games: for pushing
a red checker forward, not rushing,
just innocent, uncalculated,
resting my fingers upon the disc,
lingering over my move, anguished
about, afraid of letting go,
lest the man across from me
expertly sense the ruse,
then jump and jump and jump.

Oats

This old man, beautiful, bent, stolid,
chose years ago to boil and spoon his oats,
to brew his coffee, tend his thorns, and hear,
alone in his den, violins, fiddles
that lift him far away to Santa Fe
while he reads of Kit Carson
and draws the shawl around his knees.

Long ago, a woman like Siduri
said, "Come with me: I will build fires to warm
your bones and pour drinks to heal your wounds
and sing you melodies beyond number."

But he said, "No. This I know. Here I'll stay."

What G— Hath Wrought

You, huge-hearted man, thought
I might like Eliot books you bought,
recalling I had learned and taught
his daring, delicate poems wrought
of longing and labor, words fought
for, rhythms spoken, sung, images caught
from flashes of faith and love. I had sought
from Great Tom and from you, fine men of thought,
all any woman might want—unfraught,
unimagined riches from a man's taut
clasp opened, poured in sweetness.

Gold and Jet

Though himself never flashy,
the tall, reserved man
forever flashes gold—
he seems as good as gold.
He wears a golden ring
to tell us everything.
Ah, how he shows us
where his heart reposes.
He reminds me that at best,
when polished, I am jet,
glossy perhaps, but just jet.

No Dancing with Trees

No, please, no dancing. Impossible.
Don't ask, please. You others, go ahead:
let music twirl you into pairs
of Claudel's waltzers. May you sway and swing
and glide and glow, happy twosomes who step
giddy toward leaps of love and faith
upon a swirling floor, men's legs, black-clad,
pushing within and peeking without
the frills of pink and lilac satin, silk, chiffon.

But not for me, thank you—
I couldn't bear it.
Were he to wind me in his arms,
I'd stand lead-footed, rooted, inept,
unable to lift toe or heel,
my arms long tendrils of liana
or clematis wound tight, tight around his trunk,
my face deep in his neck, the rough bark
of brown-gray beard coarse against my cheek,
his sweet, oaken scent filling me
so that rains from my eyes alone
root us together forever.

Beyond the Glass

At kitchen table and before a hearth,
Another woman—older, wiser, white-
Haloed—taught me your shapes and names
In lines and talk.

Today, through sliding panels of my dim,
Cold house, I watch you all: six cardinals
Set aflame by lightning winter sun on snow,
Small breasts puffed out for warmth; one lone jay;
A pair of towhees; and four red-winged blackbirds,
All taking turns on the feeder ledge. Below
Snow-bellied juncos bob and flick, daintily
Pluck their seeds from snow--so small,
So frail, these little loves.

Because I shiver standing inside,
I long to hold you, save us all from cold:
I race past glass panels to embrace you,
Gather you to my shaking arms, warm you
From January zero with my coos.
But you scoot, skitter, swoop away.

Beneath, I watch you settle on safe,
Bare limbs overhead. Snowblind, I turn back
To this barren house, disappointed,
Unrequited. Like you, like her, now I see
What wise ones know: the price
Of meager warmth is light and flight.

Night Terrors

How shall I excise from my brain the worm
that burrows deep, the grub infecting
every night's vision?
Let me close my eyes to dark alone,
my arm across the second pillow,
my palm just over the imagined heart,
my face turned to receive the drowsy breath.
Let me surrender to dreamless sleep at last.
Let kind gods grant me blackout.

Instead, the brain worm mines, tunnels beneath
my reason; sapper squirming below sense,
it undermines the solid ground of hope
and bursts sweet dream into bloody death.
May the gods extirpate this hated bait
and bury it in a brainless pit.

In a flash—as from a shell—the gate of hell
blasts open, and you land
beside the loved one.
Night terrors.

Cockroach Hopes

In the dark, I disbelieve
in rosy-fingered dawns and honey-sunny days,
nights easy-breezy enough to summon
whispered secrets shared and held.
In the dark, no need for hidden hopes—
those damning, eternal cockroach hopes.
Once, they lay on the bottom of Pandora's box
till all the other evils escaped.
I see them: hard-bodied devils,
six legs kicking, antennae whickering,
even on their backs not ever helpless.

Cockroach hopes scurry across countertops,
among China plates and silver spoons,
then into secret slits between wallboard
and tile where they stock up bread crumbs
and thrive forever. They hide; they return.
Flip on the light—see them run;
let the sun rise—see them run.
After the blink and dart, they wait through day
until I forget them, think I'm safe again,
turn off the lights. But while I busy
myself disbelieving, they abide
in the dark.

Diagnosis: Hole in Heart

The patient sits up straight, waiting for doctors
who pause and ponder. Already he knows
their diagnosis, does not care to hear
another treatment option, prefers
to go on as he is, accustomed
to the hole in his heart.

The first so-called healer reiterates
that decades-old holes don't heal alone.
As if the patient doesn't know.
The healer repeats how much has fallen
inside the heart and stayed, detrimental—
as if the patient doesn't know.
Inside the heart lies laughter stanched like blood
and dreams drowned in the atrium's abyss—
as if the patient doesn't know.

The second healer has poured in gallons
of milky kindness, sewed artful sutures,
even fashioned papier-maché patches,
all cut, stripped from treasured books, the best,
most highly rated medicinal tomes.
But the pretty papier-maché patches
fell off.

The third one asks why the patient insists
on drinking vinegar, keeping the wound
raw and burning. Did the patient observe
that golden spider when it dropped and stayed

in the right atrium? Can't the patient feel
it weave its endless web to trap and choke
any rising hope? From where he stands
at the bed's foot, the healer hears and fears
the wasps' hum-squeal when they swarm
around their nest in the right ventricle,
stinging, striking, keeping the heart swelled with pain.
So many times already, Healer Three
has loosed and excised the endless web, then lanced
and lasered the fat wasps' nest, to clean and heal
those delicate, essential orifices.

In his left ventricle, blood and water
come bubbling up, boiling, seething,
to escape those piercing agonies
descending from left atrium, where, now,
at last, all see and know the worst.

Those three healers, so far failed, peer at this dread.
But not the patient who, with level eyes,
gazes across at Doctor Number Four,
the old one, poised, perhaps wise, perhaps one
to draw the cobra from its hole, let it strike
till venom all runs out. Can the old one
lay hands on that heart, persuade the cobra
to unfold, unfurl, uncoil, slither out,
then, soft palm over the patient's heart,
heal that ancient wound with warm touch alone?

Saint George and Three Dragons

Nowadays sainthood requires more, much more
than ancient Christian canonization.
Mere brave soldiering in lonely wars
against those ordinary varmints—
foul giants and evil monsters, merely
wielding magic sword and saving maiden,
well, of course, all that counts for little.
Not for sainthood. Not anymore, not now.

This modern Saint George must slay
three indefatigable dragons,
each lurking in her lair.
Show us, if you dare,
how to slay them, son of earth;
now show us bone and sinew and heart's blood.

The first creeps about her cave. She is Pain—
her name, her companion, her terror and threat.
She aches from other fights and longs to pass that ache
to some upstart like our George. No light! She hides
from daylight, prefers her dank, stinking cave
where drips of stalactites cannot balm her wounds.
She crouches, one wing folded over aching heart,
the other propping her against the ossuary
of brave knights who assailed her.
But then, oh then, when night comes,
her venom rises as of old, wings spread
but too wide for egress, and so Pain turns
inside to seethe.

When he fights Pain, if our George succumbs,
his bones will ache forever in the damp
dark of this dragon's cave.

The second, Fear, rules the desert. Her breath sears
as white and dry and quick as bursting star,
a fever burning red scar and pink scar
deep in the landscape and a knight's white flesh.
Her claws cut clean through any hero's shoulder.
Her very visage causes manly knees
to quake. But if he knows her moves, if he can feint
and dance, swoop, jab, draw her forth
until, open-jawed, she takes the lance, well
then he may win.
When he fights Fear, if our George succumbs,
his bones will lie white
and parched under the sun.

The third and deadliest foe flies overhead
from some mysterious, hideous den.
She drops sweet potions at George's door—they turn
to poison. She wafts roses' scents on summer breezes
as in former days. Her roses rot and stink. She looks ahead
while turning the knight's head behind, looking ever
back to noble feats and epic valor,
to kisses nectar sweet. Dragon Past howls
for George to grow young again, forgetful.
When he must fight Dragon Past, if we then see
viper fangs stuck in George's heart,
watch toxins drip from heart to soul, oh then,
if he succumbs, oh then, so late, if he
succumbs, his bones will crumble into dust.

Two Out of Three

For Jan
" . . . or the uncertainty of his setting forth."
W. B. Yeats, "Among School Children"

I

Behind, down the beach, two men stoop to sift
Through sand and broken shells for some relic
Of journeys in other worlds to bear away.
We two bear our relic with us
Though they don't know,
These men with whom
We come and go.

Beside our feet, sea washes in. Shells drift
Over the sand, and water-weight imprints
Their shapes—curls, pleats, spines, knobs—
their forms to stay
A minute, till the next soft wash
Of tide erases
Their printed forms,
Leaving but traces.

To scrutinize our relic's prints, we lift
Her crusted shell, brush off the sand. Below
Our fragile relic lie deep, double prints
(Her curls, pleats, spines, knobs), two exact sets
In still-damp earth—
We her daughters
Bear these forth.

II

In the May dawn, a glowing woman wades
Into the gulf. And there, as I watch, she
Begins her dance among the gleaming waves.
She spins, leaps, whirls, then rushes toward the sea;
She turns again, again—her dance I know.

Though but a solemn singer, still I share
My sister's fluid dance before the sea:
The melody that calls us, haunts us, dares
Us both to travel beyond the gulf, free,
Intones from our shell humming the sea's flow.

So I, safe on the beach, observe her twirl
Her life up to the sun, rising, leaping,
Her rhythms embracing other worlds
Than I have seen. For her turns, I'm weeping—
This dawn-dance moves me more than she can know.

Plundering Huns

Arriving from the seacoast, some Huns came
the week before she died, plundering ones
who vied with one another to lay claim
to paintings pulled from walls, Brahmin purses pried
from closets and chests, patio tables
and chairs lifted from porch and hauled
to SUVs by ageing bottle-blondes. All night
they drank, smoked, and prowled. Their fables
of ancient friendship, warmth, and love appalled
the dying woman and brought her shame.

Then breaching the walls, other Huns attacked
down telephone lines to pillage and loot
from afar. *—Let me reclaim, before you pack,*
the crystal, Neiman's heart, symbol and root
of mutual devotion. I want it back.
—Can I pick up the wine-cork birdhouse
I brought two summers ago for the back
yard? And may I take a few mementos
from her major sets of sculpted birds?

Lest she desire to languish,
the Huns enhanced her anguish.
—Devout Baptist as I am, how I prayed
with our dear sister; but once, a gift I laid
under her tree for Christmas; I'd like that back.
—Those zebras I painted, those that hang
in her second bath, just crate and ship them back.
—Last week when I left, my car's boot

*held so much that I failed to loot
the large kitchen mirror, talavera pot,
and five-piece breakfast suite. Not a lot,
but never will she need them in the crypt.
This week I can arrange to have them shipped.*
And thus the Huns plundered
while from their love she was sundered.

Noble

Of Old

In books and movies, nobles stride long-legged
down torch-lit hallways with high, arched ceilings,
boot heels and spurs a-clang upon stone floors.
They sup at tall, wood tables, in chairs
tall, even their dogs tall under their feet;
their noble knees rub tables' undersides.
They mount throwing leather-covered legs high
across horses' backs. Much in the saddle,
they ride far and wide, ford rivers, ascend
and descend mountains, besiege towns
and castles. They fight for land, or for god,
or, more likely, for daring and honor
and the pure joy of fighting.
In long gazes, nobles scan horizons,
sharp eyes looking less for foes than landmarks
signaling their scope, riches in lush lands—
in farms and forests, in lakes and rivers.
Their further riches run to outbuildings,
tools, and peasants to use them—and to horses
and weapons strong, sharp, gleaming, and wieldy.
In court and council, they hear best and worst
of human act and yearning, review laws,
weigh truths, then judge. Such men sit easily
beneath titles and ranks; receive esteem
as due, accept with nods songs and poems
of praise for their prowess and puissance,
assume their legends will live ever after.

Today

Today's noble man may wear boots and spurs,
may find his knees rub under the table,
may spend much time in the saddle, may scan
horizons here and there, now and then.
No title does he aspire to, but yearns
to fade into background, too modest
for our notice, unworthy of our time.
He never assumes, never presumes.
This noble man judges others gently
if at all, kindness falling from his hands.
His heroes save instead of slay, sacrifice
rather than demand, love rather than hate.
Of the gods he asks only little: strength
till he's ninety--to carry his saddle
and throw his leg over a horse; sharp eyes
to survey horizons—never to count
his acres, cattle, wells, but to see birds
and clouds and light; mind to find Earth's secrets.
Let the gods spare him hollow honors
so he can get on with his work and books
and horses. And doing good. Always good.
With magnanimity of mind and heart.

Orogenies

I Echidna Drakaina

Two continents long, the furious beast
awakes and stretches. Deep inside Earth scrape
and rattle her scales, miles-thick plates
protecting her reptilian nether parts.
Tail, claws, legs shove against her cramped crate,
crash after crash against her prison,
a sky god's vengeance, at earth's core.
From Echidna's dugs—which nursed Hydra,
all hundred heads; thrice-gorged guard-dog
Cerberus; Caucasus eagle with razor beak
still, even now, shredding, devouring
Prometheus's liver; other brutes
of Typhon's cursed, hideous get—
from breasts pendulous, but poisonous, leaks
an unguent viscous and gassy, torrid
so that it melts rock. Above burns her maw;
yawning, she exhales blazes hurtling through
asthenosphere and cracking lithosphere. Then
direct from Tartarus, the Hadean,
and older than Echidna's clan, erupts
her bloody magma from self-inflicted wounds.
Drakaina indeed. After millennia of sleep,
she wakes to break, crash, thrust aside
both mantle and crust, her magma loose
upon the Earth in protest of confinement.
Echidna strains, extends, expands. Amid
her curse and crash and roar, she throws

up stone and flame to spill another wash
of firerock into a mountain bed.

II *Orogenesis*

Tectonic plates slide centimeters, shift
minutely. The one, perhaps, subducts,
as in the Andes, without colliding,
beneath another, Earth's crust
rising centimeters, its lift
ensured without crash or clash, magma freed,
islands and continents born, set adrift.
Or maybe one plate meets its brother,
Laurentia with Avalonia
or Baltica, Eurasia with India—
crash, bang, thrust: rifts,
hills, mountains in genesis.
Consider Caledonian orogeny:
sometime Ordovician or Devonian
three plates met beneath
a once-current ocean: Iapetus
evaporated, disappeared while stiff,
hard plates tossed up Lewisian gneiss,
the Hebrides, Ben Nevis, and Highlands.
There Gaelic oreads danced
through crystal streams and across peaks of snow.

III *Orophony*

Orogeny, the climber says, the noun
o-shaped inside his mouth,
lips round for two syllables, teeth

closing on soft *g*, unstressed short *e*
and *y*. Treasured, loved sound:
orogeny. The climber's breath escapes
into the air, his syllables rising
as rocks rise high, and higher, to mountains.
His words bespeak noble heights. How easily
he breathes *Laurentian* and *Mont Tremblant*,
delivers *Ordovician* and *Silurian*.
He narrates other travels, other climbs
through Rockies, Sierras, Appalachians,
Laurentians again, his hearer held
tight in only his breath. Such sounds. His words
as sweet as nectar slide down those peaks
and slopes his sentences build.
The oreads dance always for him.

Palo Duro Canyon, Texas Panhandle, June 2016.
Photo by George Payne.

Sangre de Cristo Range from Capulin Volcano, New Mexico, November 2018. Photo by George Payne.

Longing for Egypt

Those Who Go

Before, centuries earlier, they came
for work and food and plenty, promises
to draw the immigrant masses. Once there,
they fired bricks and piled them, tended canals
and irrigation works, killed rats and snakes
among the stores. Some held themselves apart,
not tall enough or brown enough, not smart.
Only a few wrote or ciphered, and those
the pharaoh used inside.

But later, most of them enslaved, though still
reciting old stories of Abraham
and Lot and Noah, they forgot the god,
perhaps assuming he left them for more
admiring folk, people building temples
to him, not Osiris or Aten.
Weary of flat, arid, treeless landscapes,
they forgot how their ancestors came, long
ago, from just such a place—despite some
odd stories recounting mountains and floods,
stone cairns and pillars, even angels,
for heaven's sake. Imagine. At work, at rest,
some dozens of them wondered what lay east
across that swampy patch.

Take us out of here, Moses. Anyplace.
We hate brick-shaping and -baking; we hate

stone-cutting and tomb-building; we hate
canal-digging and desert-irrigating;
we hate rat-baning and cobra-baiting.
We'll do whatever you say. We promise.

So Moses did: he led them out. Through dust
they drudged; and across that swamp of Reed Sea
they slogged, packs of riches weighing them down,
the old tied onto their backs, the young held
on their hips, their feet slurping in the mud.
Excited, encumbered, on they trudged
behind Moses and, he said, his god,
that god of his a promise or a threat.

In early days, children raced ahead
to leap and squeal, play tag, and ignore
their mothers' calls. In early days, women
still swapped scarves, chatted, and smiled nervously
at Moses and his handsome brother.
Those early days, the elders walked upright
with their sticks and, in papery voices,
advised about travel, health, long life.
In early days, the Israelites helped
one another, sharing baskets, strong hands.
What ebullience as they swept
into Sinai, all agog at the rocks,
such awe at the mountains, miraculous
after the lifetime in flat Egypt.

But in just weeks, they became lost, burdened--
with thirst and hunger, cold and dark, no road,
no river, no clear route to Promised Land.

Some carried not freedom, but woe, misery
to sojourn in Sinai and beyond.
Such grumblings. Longing for sun-parched Egypt,
her fragrant, fragile orchards, figs and dates,
that land held together forever
by road-river Nile. Now uncertainty
and fear, regret and grief—why had they left?

Yes, years of thirst and hunger, cold and dark,
that loneliness and grief as old ones died,
young ones weakened, men and women, good friends
simply disappeared. Here one day, walking
a little behind, then just gone. No more.
And no more houses and no gardens.
Just dust and rocks.
Promised Land?
Why did they leave Egypt? Misery there
they knew and failure familiar as sand.
Why come so far, to nowhere?
Why not sneak back, hope the angry pharaoh
forgot their insolence, forbore return.
Could Egypt be home again? They'd left friends
and cousins there who might dance them back home.
Maybe those had been right all along, right
to stay at home in Egypt where they knew
what every day offered, right to ignore
mad Moses talking to god in a bush.

Those Who Stay

Under the moon Asur imagined them,
a kind, good man whose silence and sadness,

whose patient gaze they might one day recall.
Him they had dismissed for dispirit, careless
of his reticence and caution, not guessing
why he stayed behind when others raced off.
Under the cold white moon, Asur thought on
his people in the wilderness, daughters
and brothers, teachers and friends, all hurried
away from him and Egypt, all eager
for Moses's Promised Land. In a hundred years
even, Asur could not persuade himself
to surrender all he had in Egypt,
to surrender every day's certainty.
Not that Asur expected them to turn:
he'd watched the beautiful Pi-el leap, dance
away from him; Raqad skip and shriek in joy
to leave; and stern Athaq march off, somber—
not one turning for a glance back.
Awakening on the cold ground, Asur
imagined them, they stirred and rose in talk
and hurry, avid travellers ready for the road
on happy mornings.

How could Asur imagine their travail
and disappointment? How could he guess
about the long, long weeks, that golden calf,
their lack of assurance and hope? If he thought
at all on what he lost in staying safe,
Asur missed the easy talk, the circle
of sameness, the sense of being one
of many, never standing out.

Asur worked and lived on the Nile's west bank
and kept walking to the river to look
across and wonder. Could he cross and just
keep walking, catch up? Would they welcome him?
Or would they simply shun him as too late,
too fearful, too poor, coming now with nothing,
since daughters and brothers had taken all?
Thus Asur worked and lived and walked and stayed.

Raton-Clayton Volcanic Field from Capulin Volcano, New Mexico, November 2018. Photo by George Payne.

To Know

"The truth will set my city free," or so
imagined Oedipus, riddle-solver
par excellence. He strung his bow
and wholly missed the mark: hamartia.
"Just give me facts," he said; "then go
and summon those Mount Kithairon shepherds.
This day I'll brook no shrinkers, allow no
withheld facts. Today, swears blind Teiresias,
we'll name the man, end the plague, bestow
on Thebes the blessings of my brain.
Today we end this woe. Today we know."

"The truth will let us map the heavens," just so
Copernican heliocentrist,
heretical scientist Galileo
belied Urban's strictures, held scriptures
less than empirical truth. To follow
holy writ alone meant not to observe,
not to see the phases of Venus aglow,
not to hear the music of Jupiter's moons,
not to feel the Earth's tides ebb and flow.
"Let us know," he thought; "then who will maintain
Catholic, geocentric status quo?"

"What truth lies in the guilt I guess?" Just so
did Hamlet trust his gut, don inky cloak,
rebuff the king's love-you-son motto.
On dark, cold watch, could Hamlet credit

that demanding, ghostly glow
urging him to remembrance and revenge?
How distinguish devil from below
tempting Hamlet's soul to crime and sin
and king angelic stalking till rooster's crow
summoned him to penitential fires?
"Which king? Which truth? How can I know?"

"The truth can set my heart at rest," or so
believed Deianeira, hope fading,
beauty faded, love forsaken, stooping low
to ply love potion when her husband roamed.
"When Lichas set Herakles' captives in a row
for me to assess and pity, my heart
had guessed. I wanted, most of all, to know
about my husband's love. 'Tell me,' I begged,
'must I fear her? Must his wooing echo
throughout my house as he importunes her?
If you tell me, I can plan: I must know.'"

Why couldn't brainy Oedipus just slow
down with the sphinx's riddle, think beyond
four feet, two feet, three feet? Why not look below
and think not *man*, but *me*: "I, Oedipus,
the cripple with swelling feet"? Did ego
drive him on? Did Oedipal oedema?
An ancient oracle; a visit to Apollo;
a murderous sphinx; a blind, old prophet;
an hysterical wife: blow after blow
he dismissed until he knew. What shame
did truth help smart Oedipus to know?

Why couldn't stiff-necked Galileo
set down his telescope,
stop gazing out his window
at imaginary motions forbidden by the Pope?
Why not turn his head from the glow
of gorgeous Venus swimming the skies,
detach his eyes from steady tides below,
ignore how the moon plies
exact wax and wane, ebb and flow?
Had he agreed to stop his science lies,
maybe the Church could have let him know.

Had Hamlet distrusted Horatio
as he did the other college guys;
had Ghost never come to harrow
the prince's soul; had the proffered prize
Ophelia never assented (shadow
of her father in her lies) to seducing
and playing on Hamlet; had Gonzago
never died, the play reducing
a guilty king to panic, his wife to sorrow;
indeed, had nothing rotted in Denmark,
what would Hamlet need to die to know?

Why, after waiting years, would a wife bestow
her trust on love? Ignore equivocating lust
in men? Seek to silence savage, shallow
taunts about her sagging breasts, thickened waist?
Yes, her man was civilizing Greece—though
when did he ever send love, even say *love*?
A man's soul descended just how low
when he lived in and for blood?

Why didn't she foresee poison in potion, slow
and hideous burns, symbols of his lusts?
What did truth—or love—help Deianeira know?

From Aeschylus long ago
we heard *pathei mathos*: we may learn, grow
wise by suffering. If we shall know truth,
will it free us, like Oedipus, to go
alone, cursed, on three miserable feet?
Will truth from honest senses—hands, eyes, ears—
release us into years of house arrest?
Will certain gut lead us to a stage of woe
whereon die a dozen players doomed?
Or shall we trust the heart to tell us all
and learn too late we didn't want to know?

What happens to those who dare to know,
to question the old verities, to invest
their souls to heal some present woe?
What shame ensues for those who lay bare
some doom decided decades ago—
sin before original sin,
shame before original shame?
Oh, they always suffer for what they know:
some truths none of us can bear—
and with those we love,
those hideous truths we hope never to share.

Wrestling with the Angels

Our treat minder tests my patience. Some nights
she stays in the water room too long. Once
I drink my fill from the tap and fluff
my fur, she should stop that flow and come here
for treats. But on she goes—wash, wash, brush, brush,
till finally, she darks the water room and comes where
I wait on my quilt corner right under the whirr
and wind. Always in my spot. Good boy.
The menace, meanwhile, sits by the door to pounce
on any dropped bite. Not good boy ever.

Every night, she sinks on bent back legs
beside the bed to talk a while, the same
blah-blah blah-blah every night—boring:
Godsunsmoonsplanetsstars . . . pleasehelpmenot. . . .
On one shoulder I see her prim white bird,
fat, fluffy, quiet. I could catch that bird
if the treat minder kept her eyes shut.
I think the white bird whispers into her ear;
she often turns her head trying to hear.
On her other shoulder hunches the big,
luscious, glossy, black bird, who scares me, dares
me to pounce. That bird shrieks and caws
and whistles, demanding our treat minder's attention.
While on her bent legs, she tries to ignore
that black bird, turns her head aside.

At last, at last, she rises: treats coming! Four for me
but only three for the menace. Ha. After treats
and pats, we settle down for dark. Now, though,
I can tell by her sighs she listens to the black bird.
I should have eaten him. Maybe tomorrow.

In the Suburbs

Dwell I but in the suburbs
Of your good pleasure? If it be no more . . . "
    Portia, *Julius Caesar*, 2.1

For how many years does a woman dwell
but in the suburbs of a man's good pleasure?
How long will she watch for highway signs
never posted?

When will she find every attempt to swell
the measure of affection dammed: talks, walks,
long strides, amblings and ramblings obstructed
by city limits?

One day will the woman find city road—
after earthquake, tsunami, glacial melt—
all gone, every route obliterated,
bereft of path?

Table Service

How can I name his weapon? Did I miss
it in the nanosecond of my blink?
Did I feel the sweet stiletto point push
just under my rib? Did I know when
acuminated blade slid silently
through aorta and two vena cava?
All in one stroke so smooth and smart
as to elicit not even a sharp intake of breath.
Precise and deadly.

The liberator
gloved in softest suede (or maybe velvet)
deftly lifts my heart from chest to table.
Such swift, efficient work. And in that flash
my heart, entirely loosed, lies on my plate,
my own heart's blood reddening white china.
He dazzles me in innocence and skill.
My cavity empty and clean, simply
I wonder, "Will I see another beat
Or two before my bloody heart slows and stops?"

In another time and place, I might praise
his skill. But now, breathless, I sit here
at table gaping at the sliced
and served-up heart.

Arrivals

The first man's door slams
signaling entry to the basement.
Above in the kitchen, she listens, tense,
for the proverbial clichéd footstep.
Its speed will give her clues—how to stand,
how to gird, how to cover. How quickly
can she gauge the tone, guess the harangue?
Which hard words will fall first? Most nights
they bang like rocks down a steep cliff,
smacking her head and arms like a highway
below. Then larger stones drop, edges honed
into jags deep and sharp, suitable
to cut away skin, soft tissue,
to leave her bone barbed, now protruding,
white and bloody; her breath a spear
in the chest. Most nights.

The other man's door closes in a hush
so as not to disturb even the cat.
In the kitchen she listens, heart pounding,
for the proverbial clichéd footstep.
She aches over its paces, longs to hear
a rush. She stands and faces the door, silent,
hands empty, prepared to capture every word.
This night, like every other one, his words
will drop like pearls of mist in an exotic,
erotic waterfall, settling so gently
over crimson and coral blossoms

afloat below as not to burden
a petal. Every night.

In the Dark

We watch him from the lane and wait, silent
as he is silent.
In dark, outside the barn, a man gazes
down a long alley or aisle. Inside,
horses may snort softly or nicker.
We don't know.
From far away apparently, some light blazes,
illuminates the aisle's telescopic reach,
allowing him a view we cannot see.
What holds him, this man whose face
we also cannot see? Whence comes that light?
From moon or star or lamp or, more like,
from galaxies formed light years ago?
We don't know.
We see his back alone. The faraway beam
surrounds him in almost-corona.
What does he perceive? What holds him quiet
and still? Will he ever turn his face
to let us see smile or frown or grimace,
some clue to why he stands here rapt?
We don't know.
We want to see the face, to hear the heart,
to note the step. But he is far away--
and we dare not approach.
We study his back, yet offer no solace
if any is even wanted. About that, too,
we don't know.

If he turned toward the lane for a moment,
a moment only, we might catch his eye
and draw him over, engage him in talk,
learn why
he stays here. If he turned for a moment,
his face might reveal
what we don't know
and can't guess. If only he turned once,
let light from the lane illuminate him,
we might see what to do, perhaps
a hand on his shoulder,
the back of a hand soft against his cheek,
a word inviting him to walk
with us down the lane.

What Milton Knew

John Milton, *Paradise Lost* 8:48-57

Eve learned to leave the blessed bower
When Raphael called to chat. Not that angel
Politeness, charm, good manners failed to please,
Nor that his epic tale failed to thrill—such
Terrors in Eternal Father's troubles
With luminous Lucifer, who ended
In a lake of fire, still set on ruling,
If not Heaven, Hell; and then the Son,
Loving kind, yet fierce in war, perhaps
A friend to those secure, safe in Eden.
And best of all, Creation: Adam born
Of clay, and herself of Adam born.

In truth, Eve liked Raphael's tales. Better, though,
To hear them sweet from Adam's mouth. And thus
Eve left the bower to tend her nurseries.
She trimmed thornless roses, gathered sage
And basil aromatic, emptied cowslips
Of their nectar, hummed tunes in harmony
With honeybees. The sun warmed her shoulders
And pinked her cheeks. All the while Eve pondered
Her husband, pictured him rapt, as she
Herself would later be. She imagined
His questions, the angel's gentle answers.
Through the length of the still afternoon, Eve

Kept busy, aware the good angel soon
Would leave her beloved.

At last, sunlight streaking low in the west,
Eve entered the bower, her arms bountiful
With flowers, pomegranates, pistachios,
Their bouquet scenting sweet the sanctum.
Repast soon finished, Eve softly spoke, "Adam,
What story told the good angel today?"
And settling on his shoulder, Eve gazed up,
Saw Adam blush with news, secrets almost
Straight from Father Eternal.

                              Adam longed
To speak and Eve to hear his soft, low voice,
Wondrously comforting, rise and fall, breath
Of God touching her, warming her face, breath
Of her life, beloved Adam. All day
She had waited. Now his voice reminded her:
Here, indeed, is Paradise.

Another Paradise: Haskell County storm, near Sublette, Kansas, August 2016. Photo by George Payne.

About the Author

Sherry Bevins Darrell is professor emerita of English and director of Humanities at University of Southern Indiana in Evansville. She taught a variety of literature and composition courses, including Shakespeare, Milton, Greek tragedy, freshman rhetoric, and advanced composition as well as interdisciplinary Humanities.

She grew up in the Texas Panhandle and returns often to visit Texas cousins and landscapes; the photographs (and some poems) included in this volume reveal her love for the prairie.

www.ingramcontent.com/pod-product-compliance
Lightning Source LLC
Chambersburg PA
CBHW041614220426
43670CB00001B/19